FRANK LLOYD WRIGHT

FORCE OF NATURE

ERIC PETER NASH

TODTRI

This book was designed and produced by
Todtri Productions Limited
P.O. Box 572, New York, NY 10116-0572
FAX: (212) 695-6984

Printed and bound in China

ISBN 1-880908-50-6

Author: Eric Peter Nash

Producer: Robert Tod
Book Designer: Mark Weinberg
Production Coordinator: Heather Weigel
Project Editor: Edward Douglas
Editors: Don Kennison, Shawna Kimber
Picture Researcher: Ede Rothaus
Typesetting: Command-O, NYC

REFERENCES
Muschamp, Herbert, *Man About Town: Frank Lloyd Wright in New York City.* Cambridge, Massacusetts: The MIT Press, 1983.
O'Gorman, James F., *Three American Architects: Richardson, Sullivan, and Wright, 1865-1915.* Chicago: The University of Chicago Press, 1991.
Pfeifer, Bruce Brooks, *Frank Lloyd Wright.* Nuremberg, Germany: Taschen, 1991.
Riley, Terence and Peter Reed, Ed.s, *Frank Lloyd Wright: Architect.* New York: The Museum of Modern Art, 1994.
Scully, Vincent Jr., *Frank Lloyd Wright.* New York: George Braziller, Inc., 1990.
Secrest, Meryle, *Frank Lloyd Wright.* New York: Alfred A. Knopf, Inc., 1992.
Sommer, Robin Langley, *Frank Lloyd Wright: American Architect for the Twentieth Century.* New York: Smithmark Publishers, Inc., 1993.
Storrer, William Allin, *The Architecture of Frank Lloyd Wright.* Cambridge, Massachusetts: The MIT Press, 1974.
Twombly, Robert C. *Frank Lloyd Wright: His Life and His Architecture.* New York: John Wiley & Sons, 1979.
Wright, Frank Lloyd, *An Autobiography.* New York: Duell Sloan and Pearce, 1943.
The Early Work of Frank Lloyd Wright: The "Ausgefuhrte Bauten" of 1911. (New York: Dover, 1982.

CONTENTS

THE MATRIX

"Early in life I had to choose between honest arrogance and hypocritical humility. I chose honest arrogance."
FRANK LLOYD WRIGHT

Wisconsin Overture

Anna Lloyd Jones Wright, Frank Lloyd Wright's independent-minded Welsh mother, determined before her son was born on June 8, 1867, that he'd be an architect. She hung engravings of the great European cathedrals around his crib in their home in Richland Center, Wisconsin, near Madison. When the boy was seven, she gave him a set of wooden blocks devised as instructional tools for kindergartners by Friedrich Froebel. The blocks so captured the young Wright's imagination that critics have pointed out similarities between the geometric masses of the Froebel configurations and the architect's mature designs.

Wright grew up in a family steeped in religion and culture. Anna came from a line of stern Methodist ministers in Wales and her husband, William Carey Wright, whom she married one month before Frank Lloyd was born, was an indigent Baptist minister. William Wright played church organ, and Frank fondly recalled falling asleep night after night to his father's playing of Bach preludes and Beethoven symphonies. Indeed, Wright came to view music an as integral component of a room.

Another influence on the young boy was the time he spent at his uncle James Lloyd Jones's dairy farm, the Valley, where he gained an intimate appreciation of nature despite the ceaseless round of chores. In his *Autobiography*, Wright

Frederick C. Robie House
Chicago, 1910

Many critics see the Robie House as the fulfillment of the Prairie House style. The building was an amalgam of novel methods of construction and traditional elements of home. The long, low pitched roof provides an archetypal sense of shelter under its overhanging eaves, but the eaves are like nothing seen before—using welded steel supports to cantilever a full twenty feet beyond the last stone supports. The tiered balconies afford a great degree of privacy, because occupants can look outwards without themselves being seen.

rhapsodized with an artist's eye about "Night shadows so wonderfully blue . . . Wild grape, festooning fences and trees . . . The World of daylight gold."

Two more children were born to the Wrights, Jennie and Maginel, but William and Anna's marriage was an unhappy one and they were divorced in the summer of 1884, leaving the eighteen-year-old Frank as head of the household. But beware the man who has never experienced an Oedipal defeat. Wright's victory over his father in his mother's affections, and Anna's conviction that her son was predestined for greatness, helped to forge his headstrong and willful character.

The family did not have enough money to send Frank away to architectural school so he enrolled at the University of Wisconsin in civil engineering. With his mother's help, he also obtained part-time work as a junior draftsman with an engineering professor for the sum of $35 a month, some of which went toward the likes of "dancing gaiters" in order to cut a good figure on campus. Wright was already displaying his life-long proclivity for debt and high living.

During this time the architect-to-be witnessed a tragedy, that left an indelible impression on his young mind. One day he passed the new wing of Madison's old State Capitol Building in time to hear the "indescribable roar" of the building collapsing, and the "agonized human-cries" of the workers. The image of the plaster-coated men, as white as statues, emerging from the rubble with

Taliesin
Spring Green, Wisconsin, Drafting Room
Taliesin was the longest ongoing project of Wright's career. He added new structures to the estate in each decade of his nearly 70-year-long career. The house was the site of some of his deepest personal satisfactions and greatest losses. He once remarked, "Nothing picks you up in its arms and so gently, almost lovingly, cradles you as do these southwestern Wisconsin Hills."

bloodied faces never left him. The collapse was not the result of the building's architect being remiss, but was due to the contractor's having filled the core of the stout concrete piers with broken brick and rubble. Wright's buildings are all as sturdy as bedrock.

Chicago, the "Eternal City"

Wright lasted two semesters at the university, according to school records, not the three-and-a-half years he claimed in his autobiography, a small example among many of the architect's rewriting of his early years to fit the legend. After hocking his father's calf-bound copy of *Plutarch's Lives*, a set of *The Decline and Fall of the Roman Empire*, and a mink collar that belonged to his mother, he set out on a train for Chicago—or as Wright called it, the "Eternal City of the West"—with seven dollars in his pocket. He arrived on a drizzling spring evening in 1887, and for the first time saw electric lights.

After tramping the streets unsuccessfully for four days, Wright arrived at the office of Joseph Lyman Silsbee, a fashionable architect who was building a church for Wright's uncle, Jenkin Lloyd Jones. Jones, a Unitarian minister and champion of liberal causes, knew many great progressive figures of his age, including Jane Addams, Susan B. Anthony, and Booker T. Washington.

Although his uncle had forbidden Wright to quit his studies, Jones's social connections in Chicago provided a great opportunity for an up-and-coming architect. Silsbee offered young Frank his first real job in an architect's office, for the princely sum of eight dollars a week.

Fallingwater
Mill Run, Pennsylvania, 1937

Fallingwater is a profound expression of its site, with stone piers that seem to rise naturally from the surroundings, and concrete trays that mirror the ledges of the waterfall. At the same time, it is an exquisite abstract expression of a dynamic flow of space in the multiform relationships between the verticals and horizontals.

CHAPTER ONE

FOUNDATIONS

"I became a good pencil in the Master's hand."
FRANK LLOYD WRIGHT

First Commission

Chicago in 1887 was an exciting place to be a young architect. The City of the Big Shoulders fairly bristled with industry and money. A roll call of some of the newly minted millionaires gives an idea of its great worth: McCormick, Pullman, Armor, Swift, Libby. In addition, from a builder's point of view, the Great Fire of 1871, which destroyed 17,000 buildings, created a voracious demand for new fireproof buildings. The combination of small lot sizes and the development of structural iron-skeleton construction led inexorably to the creation of the first generation of skyscrapers.

In many ways, the firm of J. L. Silsbee was a congenial place for Wright to work because he was by nature suited to domestic architecture. Wright would design more than three hundred finished houses in the course of his long and varied career. Silsbee's clients were Chicago's nouveaux riches. The firm worked in the Queen Anne and Shingle Style houses that were then in vogue. Curiously, the shingled All Souls Church resembled a large suburban house. But the sacredness of home and the homelike quality of church was in keeping with Wright's upbringing. A psychologist might make something of the fact that the signature "footprint" or floor plan of Wright's Prairie House was cruciform.

Wright was always seeking a great unity of elements, the personal and the monumental in tandem. While he was with Silsbee, Wright designed his first residence, a house for his aunts at Hillside, Spring Green, Wisconsin.

The house was very much in the mold of the Shingle Style adopted by Silsbee. Wright dismissed the effort as "amateurish."

Silsbee was a first-rate sketcher, and Wright was emulous of his technique, although he noted that his first mentor seemed more interested in making pretty pictures than in the final result. Wright also absorbed the principles of *Grammar of Ornament* by Owen Jones, a leader of the British Aesthetic Movement. Jones believed that nature was the source of inspiration for architecture, a thesis Wright could relate to his raptur-

Frank Lloyd Wright House (Oak Park)
Oak Park, Illinois, 1898
Wright's home and studio in Oak Park marks the beginning of his independent career. Residential architecture would always be Wright's first love, and he continued to design houses throughout his career, which spanned seven decades. For Wright, the home was a haven against the world, and the center of family and creative activity.

Hillside Studio, Taliesin
Spring Green, Wisconsin, 1901
Wright referred to the mighty, 5,000-square foot drafting studio as an "abstract forest" of oak beams and triangular trusses. It is more than coincidental that the trusses resemble Cyclopean-scaled draughtsman's triangles. A forest of draughting triangles is an apt symbol of Wright's belief that design grows from a geometric abstraction of natural forms.

John J. Glessner House
Chicago, 1887
The boldly imaginative, forcefully individual architecture of Henry Hobson Richardson would have an enormous impact on Frank Lloyd Wright. Richardson's Glessner house was radically asymmetrical in the austere front it presented to the street and the riot of towers and windows in its inner court. It was an expression in stone of the role of the individual in public and private life.

ous experiences on his uncle's farm. Wright laboriously traced out Jones's designs, and patterned drawings after the style of the best-known Chicago architect of the time, Louis Sullivan.

With Adler & Sullivan

Before the end of 1887, Wright, who was as much a genius at self-promotion as he was at the drafting table, parlayed these drawings into a job at the firm of Adler & Sullivan. He had successfully positioned himself at the very center of the American architectural world, at the top firm in the top city.

As if by preordination Wright, who seemed to possess an impeccable sense of timing throughout his long career, appeared at a critical juncture in American architectural history. Henry Hobson Richardson, acknowledged to be the first architect to achieve a uniquely American and personal style with his massive, arched stone buildings, had died that year, just before one of his masterworks, the block-long Marshall Field Wholesale Store in Chicago, was unveiled. At the same time, Sullivan was working on the Auditorium Building, inspired by Richardson, which would nail Adler & Sullivan's reputation as the foremost commercial architects in Chicago.

Wright was hired on for $25 a week to produce drawings for the Auditorium, which would be the largest building in Chicago. Sullivan soon singled Wright out for his drawing abilities, and gave him the plum task of transferring Sullivan's sketches into working drawings. Wright, who worked with Sullivan for almost seven years and ever after referred to him as his "Lieber Meister," found Sullivan's drawings "a delight to work upon and work out."

With his new-found career success, Wright, twenty-two, married eighteen-year-old Catherine Lee Tobin, known as Kitty, on March 25, 1889.

The First Generation of Skyscrapers

Louis Henry Sullivan is regarded as the progenitor of that uniquely American structure at first called the tall office building and later commonly known as the skyscraper. Sullivan apprenticed under Frank Furness, who was evolving the vertical design typical of commercial structures in Philadelphia. Furness also influenced Sullivan with his use of geometric ornamentation derived from nature, as seen in his Pennsylvania Academy of Fine Arts buildings of 1873.

Sullivan would take this decorative element to new heights. Some critics consider Sullivan's decorative artistry to be his chief legacy as a builder, but this undervalues his contribution in pioneering the wholly American grammar of the skyscraper. In his manifesto "The Tall Office Building Artistically Considered," published in *Lippincott's Magazine* in March 1896, Sullivan wrote that the skyscraper "must be tall, every inch of it tall. . . . It must be every inch a proud and soaring thing, rising in sheer exaltation that from bottom to top it is a unit without a single dissenting line."

This aesthetic was a radical departure from the horizontal compositions of Classical and European design, and from the gorgeous yet earthbound massed stone buildings of Henry Hobson Richardson. The technological advent of the steel-framed building that replaced load-bearing masonry walls made Sullivan's vision of height possible. The change in the appearance of commercial buildings around the turn of the century is immediately apparent. Contrast the immensely thick masonry walls at the base of the Monadnock Building—the last great building made without an underlying steel structure, completed in 1892 by Sullivan's chief competitor, Daniel H. Burnham and John Root—with the airy and graceful Wainwright Building finished a year earlier by Sullivan in St. Louis, which is considered the prototype of the modern steel skyscraper.

Sullivan's achievement was mainly in articulating the façade of the building, by using narrow piers and recessed, decorated spandrels to express a sweeping verticality, in contrast to using windows as voids cut into heavy stone. The typical tall masonry building, pre-Sullivan, was built essentially like a layer cake, stacking one horizontal layer on top of another. Sullivan used the whole building to express height.

Wright was there at the inception, when Sullivan came back from a hectic walk with his solution to the problem of the Wainwright design in 1890 and dashed off a

Wainwright Building
St. Louis, Missouri, 1891

Louis Henry Sullivan, like his contemporary Richardson, rejected the prevailing architectural orthodoxies of the day. Realizing that the traditional horizontal design of a Renaissance palazzo was inappropriate for taller and lighter steel structures, he envisioned a spectacularly vertical style that became the forerunner of the American skyscraper.

sketch. "I was perfectly aware of what had happened," Wright wrote. "This was the great Louis Sullivan moment. His greatest effort. The skyscraper as a new thing beneath the sun, an entity imperfect, but with virtue, individuality, beauty all its own as the tall building was born. Until Louis Sullivan showed the way, tall buildings never had unity. They were built up in layers. All were fighting tallness instead of gracefully and honestly accepting it."

Wright's home life was as rich as his career. Frank and Kitty were about to become parents, and Wright designed a family home in the up-and-coming neighborhood of Oak Park, Illinois. Lloyd Wright was born on March 30, 1890, shortly after the house was completed. The building was in the Shingle Style. A playroom with a vaulted ceiling that Wright added five years later was more characteristic of his experiments with the inner space of houses in what came to be known as the Prairie Style.

Oak Park

Dining Room

For Wright, everything was of a unity. Even the baby's highchair here is of a piece with the overall vertical motif. Wright also continuously revised his own residences, rarely satisfied with a finished design. His associate John H. Howe once remarked of Wright's design process, "He couldn't wait to tear it down."

Guaranty Building

Buffalo, 1896

Sullivan revolutionized tall buildings by using narrow vertical piers to create a sweeping feeling of height. The gorgeously wrought spandrels, or horizontal elements of the facade, and richly decorated windows show Sullivan's unifying use of ornamentation. Wright was profoundly influenced by Sullivan's geometric expressions of natural forms.

Children followed now every one or two years—John, Catherine, Frances, David, and baby Llewelyn, born in 1903. Wright, who believed that musical appreciation was the foundation of all aesthetic understanding, gave them each musical instruments, and the Wright children made a fine six-member combo.

A rift, however, was developing between the master and his star pupil. Wright had signed a five-year contract with Adler & Sullivan in 1888 at $60 a week, but he was dissatisfied. The firm did very little residential work, preferring the big-ticket commercial projects, from which they received a percentage of the total expenditures. Wright kept his hand in domestic architecture by moonlighting—designing six houses, three for his well-to-do Oak Park neighbors. But this practice was in direct violation of his contract. When Sullivan harshly brought the matter to his attention, Wright did the unthinkable for a twenty-six-year-old architect with two children and another on the way: he quit.

William H. Winslow House
River Forest, Illinois, 1893
Wright's Winslow House shows a synthesis of the influences of his two great mentors. Like Richardson's Glessner House, Wright's building presents an austere, almost classical front to the street. The limestone frame around the door and windows is a strong echo of Sullivan's decorative philosophy, and is taken directly from Sullivan's design for the Charlotte Wainwright Tomb (1891) in St. Louis.

Winslow House
Dining Room
Unlike its public face, the private side of the Winslow House shows an exuberant use of curved, extending forms and stained glass windows. The intricate, organiform window leading strongly reflects Sullivan, while the asymmetrical massing of the elements of the house evokes Richardson.

The Prairie Style

"I don't want you to give us anything like that house you did for Winslow. I don't want to go down backstreets to my morning train to avoid being laughed at."
NATHAN G. MOORE, Wright's second client

"It comforted me to see the fire burning deep in the solid masonry of the house itself."
FRANK LLOYD WRIGHT

Wright, naturally, turned to houses in his new practice. His first commission without Sullivan was a house for William H. Winslow in River Forest, Illinois, in 1893. The Winslow House is Wright's first major synthesis of the two masters of his age, Richardson and Sullivan.

The overall plan of the Winslow House is modeled after Richardson's radically asymmetrical John J. Glessner House (1887) in Chicago. Richardson designed an L-shaped residence that literally presents two faces—a severe, balanced limestone front to the public street side, and a riot of brick towers and dormer windows on the inner, private side. Wright's Winslow House too is Janus-faced, presenting a symmetrical façade to the outside world, and protecting an exuberant jumble of porch, dormer, and wings in the back. The architect's view of the relationship between society and the nuclear family may be read into this division. Wright's debt to Sullivan can be seen in the ornamental aspect of the limestone-framed doorway, which recalls the Charlotte Dickson Wainwright Tomb in St. Louis, designed by Sullivan in 1892.

Wright's celebrated Prairie House showed a profound absorption and transformation of Richardson's and Sullivan's styles. Wright unveiled the prototype for the

Prairie House in the February 1901 issue of *Ladies' Home Journal*. The essential elements of the Prairie House are a cruciform floor plan centered around a core masonry hearth; an emphasis on a long, low horizontal line; a sheltering roof with overhanging eaves; and an open interior in which the furniture and furnishings were designed according to the aesthetics of the Arts and Crafts movement.

Richardson had much to contribute, particularly in the low, horizontal lines, and the hip roof, or four-sided sloping roof that embraces and shelters the walls with protective eaves. His Old Colony Railroad Station (1884) can be seen as a forerunner of Wright's houses. Wright would also incorporate Richardson's dynamic use of asymmetry, as in the Crane Memorial Library in

Winslow House
Interior
Wright is often credited as the creator of design movements of which he was the flower, rather than the root. There was a rich tradition of design at the close of the 19th century, such as the Arts and Crafts Movement. Wright incorporated some of the best elements of this movement—unpainted wood, natural materials, and a harmonious intergration of all the arts, from painting to sculpture, lighting, and furniture.

Wainwright Tomb
St. Louis, Missouri, 1891
Wright was profoundly influenced by Louis Sullivan's decorative style of geometric designs based on natural forms. Sullivan's design for the tomb of Charlotte Dickson Wainwright inspired the decoration of the entryway to Wright's Winslow house.

Quincy, Massachusetts (1882). Sullivan's influence on Wright is evident in the geometrical abstractions of natural forms used to decorate the interior spaces. Wright's highly stylized use of flowers, plants, and other natural forms can be traced back to Furness via Sullivan.

This synthesis was just a starting point for what Wright was conceiving inside the houses, nothing less than a transformation of interior space. Wright was the originator of the open floor plan, in which walls between traditionally enclosed spaces were eliminated. "I was working away at the wall as a wall and bringing it toward the function of a screen," Wright wrote, "a means of opening up space which, as control of building-materials improved, would finally permit the free use of the whole space without affecting the soundness of the structure."

The open plan is now such a staple of home design that it is scarcely noticed, for example a kitchen open-

Dana House

detail

Stylized sumac was the decorative motif for the Dana House. Wright was fond of using geometric abstractions of plant motifs for many of his houses, such as hollyhock for the Aline Barnsdall House, tulips for his own Oak Park residence, and the Tree of Life for the Martin House. Stained glass windows and lights give the interiors a warm and colorful glow, that like a hearth, signified home to Wright.

Susan Lawrence Dana House

Gallery, Springfield, Illinois, 1904

The Dana House was one of the grander Prairie Houses, with a double-storied gallery and vaulted ceiling. The space is adumbrated by a low, arched entranceway. Wright would come to rely increasingly on the dynamism of curved space in his later works. The Dana House is notable in that virtually everything inside was designed by Wright, including the free-standing and built-in furnishings, lighting fixtures, and the famed stained glass.

Ward D. Willits House
Highland Park, Illinois, 1903
The Willits House was another breakthrough in the Prairie Style. The massive building was divided into four wings, so that its silhouette from the street was of long, clean rooflines. Wright arranged the floorplan in a distinctive "pinwheel" formation, so that the space itself seems to flow throughout the house.

ing onto a dining area without a partitioning wall. But at the turn of the century the layout was something revolutionary. Wright called it "the destruction of the box." Suddenly rooms opened up and flowed into one another. The extended vistas between rooms, and the contrasts of low and high ceilings, gave a new spatial dynamism to the houses. Increasingly, Wright would become interested in articulating the continuity of space from room to room and from floor to wall to ceiling, as opposed to the "cut-and-butt joinery" of traditional architecture. He wrote, "Now why not let walls, ceilings, floors become seen as component parts of each other, their surfaces flowing into each other."

At the same time, the innovation of structural steel allowed Wright to open up the inside of the house to the outer environment in unprecedented ways. For example, in the Frederick C. Robie House in Chicago—which many consider the culmination of the Prairie Style—the cantilevered roof extends a full twenty feet beyond the last masonry support. The walls, which are no longer load-bearing as in Richardson's houses, are freed up to become mere glass curtains to define the

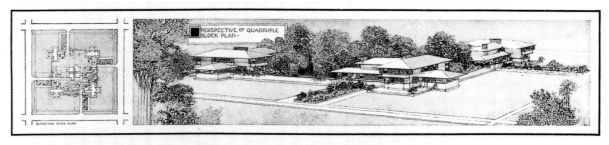

A Home in a Prairie Town
By FRANK LLOYD WRIGHT
This is the Fifth Design in the Journal's New Series of Model Suburban Houses Which Can be Built at Moderate Cost

A CITY man going to the country puts too much in his house and too little in his ground. He drags after him the fifty-foot lot, soon the twenty-five-foot lot, finally the party wall; and the home-maker who fully appreciates the advantages which he came to the country to secure feels himself impelled to move on.

It seems a waste of energy to plan a house haphazard, to hit or miss an already distorted condition, so this partial solution of a city man's country home on the prairie begins at the beginning and assumes four houses to the block of four hundred feet square as the minimum of ground for the basis of his prairie community.

The block plan to the left, at the top of the page, shows an arrangement of the four houses that secures breadth and prospect to the community as a whole, and absolute privacy both as regards each to the community, and each to each of the four.

THE perspective view shows the handling of the group at the centre of the block, with its foil of simple lawn, omitting the foliage of curb parkways to better show the scheme, retaining the same house in the four locations merely to afford an idea of the unity of the various elevations. In practice the houses would differ distinctly, though based upon a similar plan.

The ground plan, which is intended to explain itself, is arranged to offer the least resistance to a simple mode of living, in keeping with a high ideal of the family life together. It is arranged, too, with a certain well-established order that enables free use without the sense of confusion felt in five out of seven houses which people really use.

The exterior recognizes the influence of the prairie, is firmly and broadly associated with the site, and makes a feature of its quiet level. The low terraces and broad eaves are designed to accentuate that quiet level and complete the harmonious relationship. The curbs of the terraces and formal inclosures for extremely informal masses of foliage and bloom should be worked in cement with the walks and drives.

Cement on metal lath is suggested for the exterior covering throughout, because it is simple, and, as now understood, durable and cheap.

The cost of this house with interior as specified and cement construction would be seven thousand dollars:

Masonry, Cement and Plaster	$2800.00
Carpentry	3100.00
Plumbing	400.00
Painting and Glass	325.00
Heating—combination (hot water)	345.00
Total	$6970.00

IN A HOUSE of this character the upper reach and gallery of the central living-room is decidedly a luxury. Two bedrooms may take its place, as suggested by the second-floor plan. The gallery feature is, nevertheless, a temptation because of the happy sense of variety and depth it lends to the composition of the interior, and the sunlight it gains from above to relieve the shadow of the porch. The details are better grasped by a study of the drawings. The interior section in perspective shows the gallery as indicated by dotted lines on the floor plan of the living-room.

The second-floor plan disregards this feature and is arranged for a larger family. Where three bedrooms would suffice the gallery would be practicable, and two large and two small bedrooms with the gallery might be had by rearranging servants' rooms and baths.

The interior is plastered throughout with sand finish and trimmed all through with flat bands of Georgia pine, smaller back bands following the base and casings. This Georgia pine should be selected from straight grain for stiles, rails and running members, and from figured grain for panels and wide surfaces.

All the wood should be shellacked once and waxed, and the plaster should be stained with thin, pure color in water and glue.

EDITOR'S NOTE — As a guarantee that the plan of this house is practicable, and that the estimates for cost are conservative, the architect is ready to accept the commission of preparing the working plans and specifications for this house to cost Seven Thousand Dollars, providing that the building site selected is within reasonable distance of a base of supplies where material and labor may be had at the standard market rates.

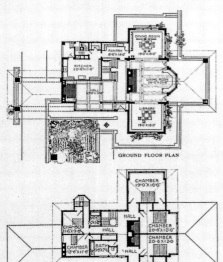

GROUND FLOOR PLAN

SECOND FLOOR PLAN

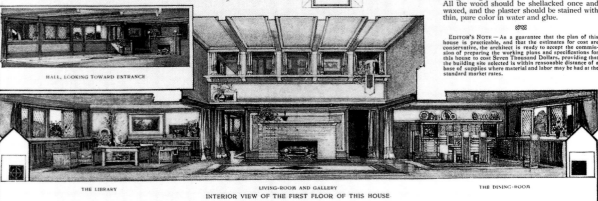

THE LIBRARY LIVING-ROOM AND GALLERY THE DINING-ROOM
HALL, LOOKING TOWARD ENTRANCE
INTERIOR VIEW OF THE FIRST FLOOR OF THIS HOUSE

17

Meyer May House

Dining Room, Grand Rapids, Michigan, 1908

Certain themes run through Wright's work like a leitmotif in music. Like a central hearth and sheltering roof, the dining room was a key center of domestic life for him. The high-backed chairs and built-in light fixtures of the table serve to create an intimate space within a space. This interior is a unified whole, from the flowers in the table planters, to the floral wallpaper, the stylized plant forms in the cupboard doors and window leading and the feathery forms in the rug.

Meyer May House

Interior

This interior is an elegant musical counterpoint between the contrasting themes of space and solidity. The lighted ceiling panels open up the roof, in the way that large windows open up the wall. The hollow wooden squares in the upper window panes are symbolic of the solid as a container of space. Solids and space are so interwoven that they become part of a continuum.

inner space and to let in light. The low-ceilinged interiors draw the gaze of the viewer out to the natural environment beyond.

But Wright's explorations in inner space are not enough to explain the near-universal appeal of his houses. At some level, the houses satisfy basic human conceptions of shelter. They are in a real sense homey, from the great sheltering roofs to the solid stone inglenooks built around a central, organizing hearth, and to the Arts and Crafts-inspired use of the beauty of natural materials in the interiors. Open floor plans, as seen from their pervasiveness in contemporary home design, are congenial to the way families actually live their lives.

Wright's achievements in the Prairie Houses—synthesizing and transcending the influences of Richardson and Sullivan in an individual, American style, creating the open plan, and incorporating new modes of construction such as the cantilevered roof—would seem enough to last several architects several lifetimes, as proved by the numerous disciples of the Prairie School. But in 1906 Wright was just preparing for the works that would come to be regarded as his masterpieces.

Willits House
Interior

Wright's houses are designed so that the smallest change in vantage point results in a fresh experience of the space. The Willits House in particular expresses a Transcendentalist unity from the greatest to the smallest parts. The basic plan of long, rectangular rooms is repeated contrapuntally in the sleek window leading, the vertical chair backs, and even in the narrow slats of the floorboards. As with any great work of art, new connections are revealed over time.

CHAPTER TWO

THE NEW REALITY

"The space within became the reality of the building."
FRANK LLOYD WRIGHT

Mold clay into a vessel;
From its not-being (in the vessel's hollow)
Arises the utility of the vessel.
LAO-TZU

The Larkin Building

Wright made a quantum jump in manifesting his conception of interior space with the Larkin Company Administration Building in Buffalo in 1906. The city leveled the structure in 1950, in keeping with misguided notions of civic progress that preferred parking space to old buildings, but photographs confirm its significance to the history of twentieth-century architecture.

From the outside, the clifflike brick towers resemble nothing so much as battlements. In a technique that Wright employed repeatedly in his houses, the entrance is at first difficult to discern, hidden in a dark space next to a more visually prominent fountain. Upon entering, one went from daylight into a dark, low, and mysterious corridor. To one side, light beams down beckoningly between massive piers. Even a keen observer was unprepared for the sudden upward rush of the vast, skylit interior. All employees worked together in the open floor plan, with balconies above and a rooftop restaurant, from which the ferns and flowers could be seen from the court below. The building thus becomes a vast container of the interior space. Wright extolled "the new reality that is *space* instead of matter."

The Larkin Building contained many innovations. It was one of the first air-conditioned buildings in the United States, employing blocks of ice. It was the first building to use plate-glass windows and doors. There

were good reasons to keep the building hermetically sealed from the outside—nearby trains from the New York Central line belched black smoke into the air. Wright conceived of the building as a "great fireproof vault." Even the furniture was made out of stainless steel, another first. A surviving example of a chair at the Metropolitan Museum looks, with its swivel base, like the very prototype of the modern office chair.

Larkin Building
Atrium Court
A visitor to the Larkin Building would experience a hieratic movement through space, from the long, long entranceway under heavy masonry walls to the unexpected uprush of space and light in the glass-ceilinged atrium that ran the entire height of the building. Wright delighted in startling the viewer to attention with sudden transitions in volume of space.

Unity Temple
Oak Park, Illinois, 1908
Unity Temple is composed of massive, abstract blocks in concrete, giving little clue, at least in the American vernacular tradition, to its function as a church. The visitor is led through a low, mazelike entrance to experience the unexpected double-storied space within.

Larkin Company Administration Building
Buffalo, 1906
The Larkin Building and its contemporary, Unity Temple, mark another major evolution in Wright's understanding of interior space. Wright often spoke of the importance of matching a structure to its site, but this building, set in a gritty industrial section of Buffalo, seems to turn its back on the environment to create its own space within. Geometric masses nearly unbroken by windows, with little visual cue to the entranceway, present a somewhat forbidding front to the street. The massive walls contain a breathtakingly open, light, and airy interior.

Unity Temple
Skylights
Wright used lighting of all kinds—built-in fixtures, lamps, stained glass windows, and ceiling panels—to guide and define the viewer's experience of space. Warmly tinted skylights add to the sense of a serene and sheltered space. Set within deep coffers, the skylights are a marvelous interweaving of space and solids.

Unity Temple

Wright embraced the newest materials and building methods. His Unity Temple in Oak Park was the first major building executed entirely in poured concrete. Wright seemed to want to build a church unlike any other church in America yet still make it true to its function as a place of worship. The outer walls of the cube-shaped building are monolithic and somewhat forbidding expanses of concrete, unbroken by any windows at ground level. In contrast to the traditional steeple the Unity Temple had a flat roof. Wright's concept in the plan, he wrote, was to "Let the room inside be the architecture outside."

The mazelike entry, hidden in the rear, is once again a dramatic preparation for the climactic revelation of the interior. The main meeting room is one of Wright's most glorious inner spaces. Daylight filters down through warm amber-colored skylights recessed in deep coffers in the ceiling and from the ornamental clerestory windows that link wall and ceiling in a profusion of light. Wright subsequently jotted on a drawing for this structure: "The unlimited overhead. Interior space enclosed by screen-features only. Idea later used in Johnson Building, Racine, Wisc."

By 1905 Wright was working on no less than thirteen new commissions. He continued to explore variations of the Prairie Style, making design advances on

Unity Temple

Interior

Unity Temple is an expression of Wright's belief in the sacredness of space and the importance of wholistic design. The shape of the building directly expresses and contains the space within. Amber-colored skylights and the concrete walls serve to remove and insulate the space from the ordinary world.

all fronts, notably in the Darwin D. Martin House (1904) in Buffalo, built for his patron, who was the chief executive officer of the Larkin Company. The Martin House is known for its beautiful "Tree of Life" patterned glasswork. Robie House (1910) in Chicago, also part of this extraordinarily creative period in Wright's life, is also known for its innovative furniture, especially the high-backed dining chairs and lamps on pylons built into the corner of the dining table, which serve to create an intimate space within a space.

The explosion of creative energy may have led to the dissolution of Wright's home life. In 1909, for reasons that still elude his biographers, he walked out on Kitty and their six children, as well as on his burgeoning architectural practice, to begin an affair with the wife of one of his clients. It was one of the great scandals of the age. When Wright slipped off to meet his paramour, Mamah Borthwick Cheney, in Berlin, the *Chicago Tribune* plastered the story across the front page on November 7 of that year.

Wright came back from Berlin and Fiesole, Italy, a year later to make a token reunion with his wife, but the marriage was effectively over. Wright found himself a pariah among his bourgeois Oak Park neighbors. He fled back to the arms of his mistress and the charms of the Tuscan countryside, where he planned his own hillside residence, to be built near his family back in Spring Green, Wisconsin.

Taliesin

Taliesin ("shining brow," in Welsh), completed in 1911, would be the site of Wright's principal residence for the next fifty years, until the end of his life. The Chicago papers wrote about the "love nest" that Wright was building for the notorious Mrs. Cheney. Unfazed, Wright continued with construction of Taliesin, a melding of his own Prairie Style with elements of the Villa Medici.

Like the Villa Medici, Taliesin was situated on the brow of a hill, with protected, walled gardens. Wright's need for haven and refuge from a critical outside world can be read into the sheltered quality of the design. Limestone for the walls, courts, and terraces was taken from a quarry a mile away; thus the house appears to be of a piece with the hill and the ground. Low-tiled hip roofs traced the lines of the hill, punctuated by taller limestone stacks. Broad casement windows surveyed the slopes. From below, the house seemed to hug the hill. Wright decorated the inside with his extensive collection of Chinese pottery and sculpture and Momoyama screens.

Taliesin was an eloquent summation of Wright's beliefs about the organic unity of man and nature. He codified his evolving theory of what he termed "organic architecture" in a 1908 article for *Architectural Record*. There were six chief points to organic architecture: first, that it be a design of simplicity and repose; sec-

Taliesin

Living Room

The living room at Taliesin commanded panoramic views of the surrounding Wisconsin countryside. Wright lived very much in the baronial manner at his estate, holding live concerts by the huge hearthside (at right), as he sat surrounded by his family with the obligatory collie at his feet.

Taliesin

Spring Green, Wisconsin, 1911

Taliesin, meaning "shining brow" in Wright's ancestral tongue, Welsh, was very much influenced by his visit to the hillside Villa Medici in Fiesole, Italy with his mistress, Mamah Borthwick Cheney. The house was twice destroyed by fire, and the extant structure is often referred to as Taliesin III.

ond, that it expresses the owner's and the project's individuality; third, that the site is incorporated in the design elements; fourth, that the colors be drawn from nature; fifth, that the building is true to the nature of the materials; and sixth, that the building express a spiritual integrity. Wright would proceed to bend most of these precepts beyond their logical conclusion over the course of his career, but blind consistency was never his strong suit.

Wright's practice suffered, perhaps as a result of his notoriety and his distance from the commercial hub of Chicago, but events more tragic and inconceivable were soon to follow.

Midway Gardens

In 1913 Wright had only three commissions. One of them, however, was grand enough to occupy his prodi-

gious energies. Midway Gardens (1914), in Chicago, was a megalithic restaurant and beer garden that took up an entire city block. The architect was involved in every detail from the construction of the massive towers, pavilions, and terrace to the minutiae of designing plates and menu covers. The structure was uncharacteristically playful for a Wright creation, with sculptures of "sprites" smiling beneficently over all, but well in keeping with the festive atmosphere of a beer garden.

Wright saw the whole enterprise as an experiment in ever more abstract and geometric forms, after the apparent death knell for the art nouveau movement in France. The Gardens went broke during Prohibition, was briefly used as a skating rink, and then was torn down to put up a laundry. Wright took a grudging satisfaction when, because his building was so solidly constructed, the removal contractor lost money on the job.

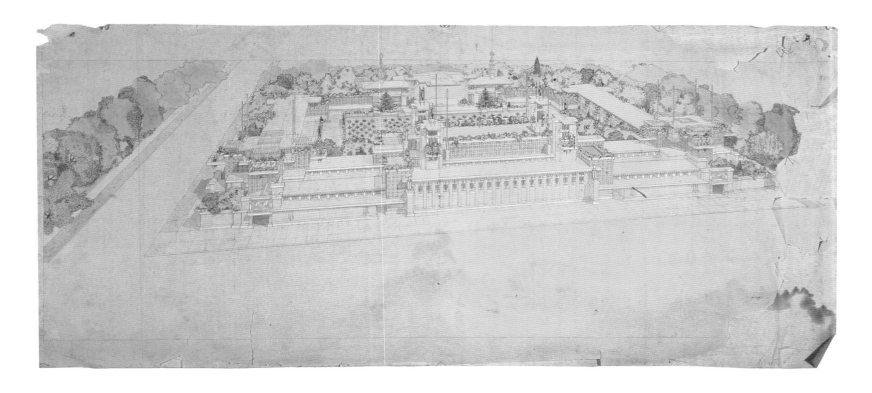

Taliesin
Interior

Taliesin was Wright's principle residence for almost 50 years, and reflects the man in every aspect. Today in addition to being an active architectural fellowship, Taliesin contains one of the most extensive collections of Frank Lloyd Wright furniture in the world. During his life, the estate served as Wright's own best advertisement—when he wanted to impress clients, he invited them out to Taliesin.

Midway Gardens
Chicago, 1914

Midway Gardens was one of the more fantastical of Wright's creations, both in its scale and in its fanciful details. The concept was to create the holdiay atmosphere of a German outdoor beer garden. Wright designed everything from the benignly smiling "Sprite" statuary that looked down on the revelers to the murals, plates, and menus. Midway Gardens took up an entire city block, but the passage of Prohibition in 1919 effectively brought an end to such establishments, and after reincarnations as a garage and a car wash, the wrecking balls were brought out in 1929.

Phoenix from the Ashes

At noon on August 15, 1914, Wright was eating lunch at the newly finished bar of the Gardens when he got a call that Taliesin had been destroyed by fire. The rest he learned from the headlines on his train trip home. A servant at Taliesin named Julian Carlton went berserk and killed Mamah and her children John and Martha with a hatchet. He then set the house ablaze with gasoline. In half an hour the residential part of Taliesin had burned down to the ground and stonework. Only the tall, blackened chimneys were left standing; the studio was spared. Seven died in the tragedy. Carlton was caught, and two months later starved himself to death in jail.

Wright cut down Mamah's garden to fill her coffin with flowers. She was buried without church services in an unmarked grave. Wright wrote, "All I had left to show for the struggle for freedom of the last five years past that had swept most of my former life away, had now been swept away."

Wright fought an overwhelming sense of despair by throwing himself into the work of rebuilding. He altered the plan where it most reminded him of the loss, and added a guest wing so his mother and aunts could live with him. Taliesin II was completed late in 1915. The house burned again in 1925, in a blaze so hot that plate-glass windows melted into pools. Undaunted, Wright took up the work of building Taliesin III, adding shards of his beloved Tang sculptures and Ming pottery to the cement for the masonry.

Providentially, as the United States was entering the great conflagration of World War I, Wright got just what his tormented spirit needed—a new love, a grand project, and a change of scene. The construction of the Imperial Hotel in Tokyo, which endured earthquakes and fire, would occupy the next six years of Wright's life. He also had a new mistress, Maude Miriam Noel. She was a rather melodramatic personage from an old Southern family, who had written him a sympathetic letter about the tragedy. In her perfervid correspondence she expressed unabashed adoration for Wright—"Lord of My Waking Dreams!", she greeted him in one letter. The great architect was susceptible to such flattery. He

fell in love. Miriam moved into Wright's small home at 25 Cedar Street in Chicago, and together they set off for Tokyo.

The Imperial Hotel

Wright could be counted on to do the unexpected. His showpiece in Tokyo, the Imperial Hotel (1923) was a most un-Japanese building. He had experimented for years with Japanese-style roof lines, notably in the strong horizontals and overhanging eaves of the Robie House, but the roofs of the Imperial Hotel were flat slabs. He abandoned wood and plaster for reinforced concrete. Even Japanese-style roof tiles, which Wright had used in so many houses, were discarded for copper. This was part of his plan to make the building earthquake-proof, because tiles became flying projectiles when buildings collapsed.

Instead of austere, plain wall panels that receded into the building's overall composition, the walls of the Imperial were made of elaborately carved soft lava blocks and brick. Japanese houses were traditionally construct-

Following page:
Hollyhock House
Wright was off on his own in the 1920s, pursuing a pre-Columbian vision, while the rest of the architectural world, spearheaded by Mies and Le Corbusier, sought to do away with ornamentation. Wright's work from this period does not seem so eccentric from the viewpoint of post-modernism. One can only note how fine the broad white planes of concrete look against the green space, punctuated by the decorative hollyhocks.

The Imperial Hotel
Tokyo, Japan, 1923
The Imperial Hotel was another phantasmagorical project. At a time when the Bauhaus architects such as Ludwig Mies van der Rohe and Walter Gropius were stripping buildings down to their most abstract essentials, Wright went the other way, back to the picturesque. The sprawling hotel was a funhouse of unusual vantage points, idiosyncratic spaces, massive ornamentation, and picturesque views. It survived the Kanto Earthquake of 1923, but not the vicissitudes of the Japanese real estate market, and was torn down in 1968. The original entrance lobby was dismantled and restored at Meiji Village, near Nagoya, Japan.

Aline Barnsdall House, (Hollyhock House)
Los Angeles, 1921
If ever a building was suited to the environment of Hollywood, it is the grandly theatrical Hollyhock House, named for its geometrically stylized motif of hollyhock flowers. Once viewed as an operatic aberration to Wright's main body of work, the California houses are receiving new critical attention for their boldly visionary use of interior space. The scale of Wright's vision and ambition did not falter, even as critical attention turned away from him in the 1920s.

ed of wood and paper to be lightweight in that earthquake-prone land. Wright instead opted for a temple of reinforced concrete. He turned for inspiration to something he had been working out with the Midway Gardens—the massive stone temples of pre-Columbian architecture, such as the Temple of the Two Lintels at Chichén Itzá in the Yucatán. Echoes of this massive cube shape can be seen in Wright's earlier A. D. German Warehouse (1920) in Richland Center, Wisconsin. Wright sought a similar monumentality, scale, and sculptural mass in the Imperial Hotel.

The hotel was as much of an engineering feat as an architectural task. The site was essentially a giant mud bank, with eight feet of "cheeselike" soil atop more than sixty feet of soft mud. Wright arrived at the solution of a floating foundation, which originated in Chicago, where unstable foundations of clay and sand were prevalent. He made the analogy of a "building made as the two hands thrust together palms inward, fingers interlocking and yielding to movement."

The weight of the building would be spread out over a series of concrete pins imbedded in the earth, so that the building would "float" on the pad of mud like a battleship on the ocean. The floors were cantilevered from central supports, much the way a waiter's fingertips hold up a tray. Sections of the building were jointed together for flexibility. The walls, in contrast to traditionally top-heavy Japanese architecture, were heavy at the base to keep the center of gravity low. All the plumbing and wiring was laid in separate concrete trenches, clear of the foundations.

Wright's backers balked at the escalating construction costs, but a fire and then in April, 1922, the worst earthquake in three decades, brought them over to his side. The building also survived the Great Kanto Earthquake of September 1, 1923, the worst earthquake in Japan in this century.

The California Houses

By pursuing his decorative, neo-Columbian designs in the Imperial Hotel, and in the five "California Houses" of this period, such as the Aline Barnsdall Hollyhock House (1921) and the Charles E. Ennis House (1924), Wright was flying in the face of the prevailing wind in international architecture, emanating from Europe. Le Corbusier in France, and the leaders of the Bauhaus school in Germany, Walter Gropius and Mies van der Rohe, were preaching a new aesthetic of the machine-age.

Followers of the Bauhaus or International Style that it evolved into, took Sullivan's dictum that "form follows function" to its most reductive sense. Anything decorative was relegated to the trash heap of history. Gropius, the great minimalist, said "less is more." To Le Corbusier the house was "a machine for living." Wright's work in the 1920s was the antithesis of this

Hollyhock House
Living Room
The embattled architect of the 1920's seemed to be returning to the most basic elements of earth, air, fire, and water. An evening soiree around the fireplace at the Hollyhock house could have been a scene right out of Wagner's "Siegfried," with starlight shining down through the skylight and a roaring fire within a massive hearth reflected in the pool of water. Wright seemed in search of a new myth to reinvent himself in the next decade.

Ennis House
Interior
The interior of the Ennis House is spectacularly dynamic. Fractional changes in vantage point create vast new connections between the rooms. The viewer becomes acutely aware of relations between volumes of space, as the rooms shift abruptly from long horizontals to steep verticals. Space itself seems to take on a kind of substance or tangibility by virtue of this flowing relationship.

Charles E. Ennis House
Los Angeles, 1924
The Ennis House, which
dominates its hillside site like
a Mayan temple, was constructed of modular, patterned concrete blocks that Wright called
the textile block system. The
system was meant to be inex-
pensive and durable, but the
concrete material was later
discovered to be porous and
vulnerable to damage from
rainwater and acidic smog.
Some of the buildings are
in dire need of restoration.

approach. Where the Bauhaus sought to articulate the pure function of a building, like Gropius's pristine glass cubes, Wright went for razzle-dazzle theatrics, such as in the epic Hollyhock House fireplace, surrounded by a moat and topped by a skylight.

The Bauhaus school stripped away superfluous decoration; Wright loaded it on, as in the dominant patterns of concrete block in the Ennis House. The Bauhaus held up the useful as the good; Wright appeared like a throwback to the nineteenth century, with his picturesque nooks, crannies, and lookouts in the Imperial Hotel. The Bauhaus sought to sever all references to a dead past; Wright consciously evoked pre-Columbian grandeur.

The 1920s were not kind to Wright. Many commissions, like his 39-story National Life Insurance Company building in Chicago with its innovative core and cantilever structure, were never built. Other than the Arizona Biltmore Hotel in Phoenix (1927), he executed only a handful of commissions—one for himself, another for a cousin, and one for his old patron Darwin Martin. In the United States, he was beginning to be seen as a bit of an anachronism, a holdover from a much different era. Even the thought of such a thing was intolerable to Wright.

In addition, Wright's home life was once more in upheaval. He married Miriam in November 1923, the

Mrs. George Madison Millard House (La Miniatura)
Pasadena, California, 1923
The Millard House, better known as La Miniatura, somehow manages to be both intimate and colossal in scale. The house is unusual for Wright in that the emphasis is on the vertical line, rather than the horizontals that characterize so much of his work. Wright's use of concrete blocks reinforced with steel rods was part of his ceaseless experimentation with new materials and construction methods.

Ennis House
Library
Voids, or negative spaces, themselves create a sense of flow within the Ennis House. Here, the different widths and heights of the window and door openings make the viewer aware of the multifaceted relationships between the spaces. The leaded arrowtip shapes in the windows give a dynamic flow to the surfaces, while the doorway draws the eye into the depth of the space.

John Storer House
Hollywood, California, 1924

Storer House

Floor-to-ceiling windows, an elegant hardwood floor
and Prairie Style furnishings soften and humanize the
interior of the monumental-looking concrete house.
The California houses, though a departure from the Prairie
Style, still feature such Wright hallmarks as a central,
anchoring hearth and advantageous views of the outside.

Wright's California houses give a sense of space in motion. The
tall textured concrete piers draw the eye up and outward, only to
be brought back to the slender diagonal of the colorful pool. At the
same time, windows in a far wall attract the viewer to the interior
of the building. The whole composition is as vibrant as the patterns
on the textile blocks. Wright referred to his California houses
as "a holiday in Romanza," using the term for a musical fantasy.

month his divorce from Kitty became final, and less than a year after his mother Anna had died. Miriam was a longtime morphine addict (a legal habit until 1914) and her moods became increasingly unstable. Later, in her divorce petition, Miriam charged that Wright had beaten her. Wright did not contest the claim. After their divorce was finalized in 1928, Wright wrote to her "whatever was in me for you is absolutely dead." It is easy to read Wright's embattled state of mind into the perdurable concrete fronts of his California Houses.

It is a mistake, however, to think that the California residences are somehow lesser projects, or that Wright's creative spirits at this time were flagging. If anything, he achieved a new level of richness and complexity in the interior space of the Ennis House. One enters the house like an acolyte, through an oppres-sive, low-slung corridor, and a twisting stairwell which was likened to a cave passage. The journey is hieratic, ritualistic. After a turn at the top of the stairs, the sight of the long, bayed loggia is overwhelming. The space demands penetration, exploration. Unexpected experiences await.

Stepping into the living room provides one with an entirely new orientation to the house, as the ceiling reaches up twenty-one feet. The columns afford startling interior vistas from room to room. As in the most magnificent of his houses, the space is alive, in constant motion.

Despite the setbacks of the 1920s, Wright could never be counted out of the architectural picture. It was time once again to reinvent himself. In the 1930s he did just that, returning like a force of nature to create perhaps his greatest works.

Arizona Biltmore Hotel
Phoenix, Arizona, 1927
The Arizona Biltmore Hotel is more of a Wright-style building than a first-hand creation. The hotel was designed by Wright's apprentice Albert Chase McArthur, and Wright served as consulting architect. The exact nature of the collaboration is the subject of vigorous debate, but nonetheless the hotel offers the public the rare opportunity of experiencing what it is like to live in a Wright space. Perhaps Wright's apprentices by and large did not achieve great renown on their own because the Master's imprint was so strong.

Arizona Biltmore
Interior
The walls of the hotel consist of 250,000 textured concrete blocks, cast from local sand, that make the interiors seem to glow from within. Wright was so inspired by the desert environment that he later went on to build one of his masterpieces, Taliesin West, in nearby Scottsdale.

CHAPTER THREE

FORCE OF NATURE

Tao is a hollow vessel,
And its use is inexhaustible!
Fathomless!
Like the fountain head of all things.
LAO-TZU

"Space. The continual becoming: invisible fountain from which
all rhythms flow and to which they must pass. Beyond time or infinity."
FRANK LLOYD WRIGHT

Olgivanna

Wright's personal redux dates to August 25, 1928, when he finally broke free of his poisoned relationship with Miriam, and married a comely divorcée half his age from the tiny country of Montenegro named Olgivanna Hinzenberg. Ever impulsive, Wright met Olgivanna in November 1924, and fell in love as quickly as he had with Miriam. Olgivanna moved into Taliesin after the new year, and a daughter, Iovanna was born to them on December 2, 1925. The wedding invitation bore a picture of Iovanna, then three years old.

Olgivanna was just the woman to promulgate the career and legend of Frank Lloyd Wright. She was a votary of George Ivanovitch Gurdjieff, a charismatic, Armenian-born mystic who founded a philosophy of spiritual development based on physical and psychological disciplines designed to awaken his followers from what he termed mankind's profound slumber. Olgivanna lent her considerable energy and organizational skills to founding, in 1932, the Taliesin Fellowship for Wright's apprentices.

Four commissions finished in the late 1930s put Wright back on the map of world architecture, not as a page from the history books but as a living force, and consolidated his reputation for future generations. In reaction to the hegemony of the International Style, Wright went back to first principles of geometric forms and abstraction. In fact, a 1910 work of Wright's, published in Germany and called *Ausgeführte Bauten und Entwürfe von Frank Lloyd Wright*, had been a critical influence in pushing the young Bauhaus designers in this direction. Wright wanted to show them that he still had a trick or two up his sleeve.

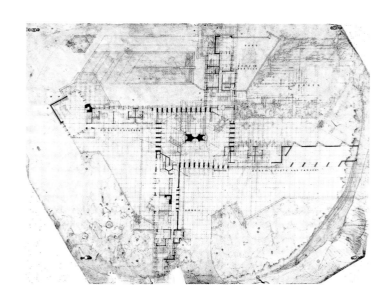

Edgar J. Kaufmann House (Fallingwater)
Mill Run, Pennsylvania, 1937
Fallingwater, a word that happens to contain Frank Lloyd Wright's initials, is perhaps the best-known private residence in the world. The house became an icon of modern design, even satirized in a New Yorker cartoon with a row of identical Fallingwaters, and put Wright back in the center of American architecture. In a sense, Wright was playing a game of one-up-manship with his Internationalist rivals, by incorporating Mies's floating abstract planes into a building so site-specific that it could only be a part of the American Transcendentalist vocabulary.

Wingspread
Floor Plan
Wingspread's huge 14,000 square feet of floor space is arranged in four, one-story wings in a cruciform pattern around a central, two-story living room with skylights. The wings function as a concretization of the pinwheeling sense of space within the Prairie Houses.

Fallingwater

Fallingwater presents a myriad of moods, depending on vantage point, season, and time of day. The house is a triumphant unity of opposites— the cool, abstract planes of concrete contrasted with the warm interior lights; the naturalistic piers of native stone merging with the abstract geometry of the horizontal trays; and the interplay of open glass spaces with masonry solids. Fallingwater achieves a sense of dynamic repose.

Fallingwater

Fallingwater (1937) is a culmination of Wright's use of abstract, geometric forms and a mature expression of his philosophy of man's place in nature. The house fully incorporated the natural setting of a waterfall in Mill Run, Pennsylvania, in a way that was totally unknown to proponents of the International Style. Think of Corbusier's Ville de Savoie, which would carry equal weight on almost any greensward on earth; Fallingwater, on the other hand, would be inconceivable anywhere else.

The client, Edgar J. Kaufmann, wanted the house positioned downstream, with a view of the falls, the locale from which the best-known photographs of the house are taken. Wright convinced him to locate the house directly over the falls, to use the flowing stream in an unprecedented synthesis of nature and design. From below, Fallingwater appears as pure abstraction. The cantilevered concrete slabs shoot off in all directions. It is neither a vertical nor a horizontal design, but more like an outcrop of the living rock. The house is a sculpture in space, changing as the point of view changes.

Wright's Fallingwater is a unity of opposites. All of the architect's great themes find expression here. He had found a synthesis of the seemingly conflicting strains of Romanticism and Modernism in his work. Fallingwater quite simply utilizes both disciplines, one blending into the other. The house is firmly in the Romantic tradition, with its picturesque natural setting and use of native materials, yet it is also a thoroughly modernist structure, with its asymmetrical and cantilevered concrete trays seemingly floating in space. The transition of rock ledge to fieldstone supports to concrete planes manifests Wright's belief, traced back to Sullivan and Furness, that design is a geometric abstraction of nature. This is where Wright diverged from the chilly abstractions of the modernists. Fallingwater looks as if it belongs in nature.

The house is a dialectic between natural and sculptural forms; between the anchored and the free-floating; between variety of materials and repetition of form; between stasis and movement; between shelter and precariousness; between unity and separateness. The great themes can be seen in the smallest details of the construction. For example, the dialectic nature of the man-made and the natural is visible in the way that glass and steel directly abut the fieldstone walls. The duality of interior and exterior from the rooms to the terraces is resolved with continuous planes of concrete walls and flagstone floors without thresholds. The hearth is situated on living rock that extrudes more than a foot through the floor.

The effect is primitive—a romantic refuge in the heart of a truly modern exterior. The house seems ready to fly in different directions yet rests in a dynamic repose. The genius of the house is that space becomes plastic, continuous, and visible, almost like the stream of water itself.

Fallingwater
Living Room
The open living room, which measures thirty-five by forty-five feet with views on all sides, is an elegant synthesis of the dialectic between nature and civilization. The hearth was built directly on living rock, which extrudes into the floor. The quarried stone floor leads uninterruptedly outside past the glass doors, and the low ceiling provides a sense of shelter even though the glass walls are open to outside. Fallingwater is an expression of Wright's Transcendental view of the deep harmony between nature and humankind.

The Johnson Wax Administration Building

The Johnson Wax Administration Building (1939) was an inversion of Fallingwater, and a breakthrough for Wright on several fronts. Instead of a spectacular natural setting, the site for the new company headquarters was a dismal industrial lot in Racine, Wisconsin. Like the earlier Larkin Building, the Johnson Building turned its back on the environment in order to look inward. Wright called the building "an up-to-the-minute thoroughbred, daughter of the Larkin Building." Only this time, Wright took the creation of interior space a step further, almost to the point of creating an artificial reality.

The Johnson Building makes its intentions known from the outset. There are no conventional windows as such, just a sleek band of translucent Pyrex tubing above head level and, most electrifyingly, where the walls meet the roof. The glass cornice announces boldly that the walls are not load-bearing but used instead to define space. Wright adopted the then-current vogue of streamlining, rounding off all the corners and giving the building a sleekly abstract, undulating shape.

Perhaps the design originated in Wright's first meeting with company president, Herbert F. Johnson, when the two men shouted at each other the whole time, agreeing only that they both owned a streamlined Lincoln Zephyr. Or perhaps Wright's turn to streamlined curves was an announcement to the architectural world that he was as up-to-date as any of his contemporaries. But the plan was a radical departure for Wright—from the severe rectangular forms he had based his career on to the use of the circle and curve as basic forms. Wright would use circles, arcs, and hemicircles with increasing aplomb, in the Robert Llewellyn Wright residence (built for his son in 1953), and culminating in the inverted ziggurat of the Guggenheim Museum and the extraterrestrial ovals of the Marin County Civic Center in San Rafael, California.

Wright uses the device of a hidden, low entrance to prepare the observer for the hieratic journey into what is called the Great Workroom. The 230-square-foot chamber is nothing less than an artificial environment. There is no sense of being enclosed within a room, as the glass cornice destroys the box. The space is defined by ninety columns that Wright

Johnson Administration Building
Great Workroom

As in the Larkin Building, employees work side by side in a
continuous, open ground-level space. Lighting is provided
by bulbs behind a ceiling made of miles of Pyrex glass-tubing,
supported by the famous "lily-pad" concrete columns. A smooth band
of glass at the level of the cornice reinforces the impression that the
ceiling is floating in space. Much has been made of
the Minoan influence on the shape of the columns, but they
also resemble nothing so much as the wooden bobbins used
in textile mills at the beginning of the Industrial Revolution.

called "dendriform." The twenty-one-foot tall hollow columns are made of concrete reinforced with steel mesh, and taper down to delicate nine-inch-in-diameter feet, shod in bronze holders. Atop the column are twenty-foot-in-diameter "pods" that support the skylight of glass tubing. The effect can be likened to lying at the bottom of a still pool and gazing up at the light filtering down from the surface, past giant lily pads. Wright progressed so far in his search for a geometric expression of nature that he had created his own environment.

The building was an immediate success. *Life* magazine,

in May 1938, rhapsodized about the interior, "It is like a woman swimming naked in a stream, cool, gliding, musical in movement and manner." Wright followed up the commission with a residence for H. F. Johnson. Wingspread, which employed sweeping curvilinear horizontal forms much like the Marin County Civic Center, was the largest and last of the Prairie Houses. In 1950 Wright added a fourteen-story curved brick-and-glass research tower to the Johnson Administration Building. Anchored by a cantilevered core, the tower seems to float on its glass screen.

S.C. Johnson & Son, Inc. Administration Building
Racine, Wisconsin, 1939

The Johnson Administration building is a triumphant reinvention of the principles used in the Larkin Building. Like its predecessor, the Johnson Building turns its back on its drab, industrial setting, to create a magical, enclosed space within. The continuous lines of the sleekly streamlined exterior are an expression of the prevailing aesthetic of machines and progress in the 1930s. The unusual, cantilevered 14-story research tower, left, was completed in 1950.

Johnson Administration Building
Entrance

The entrance to the Johnson Administration Building is a marvelous counterpoint of circular solids and voids that anticipates the flow of space in the Great Workroom. The "lily pad" circles are echoed by the concave hemicircle of the upper balcony and the convex curve of the lower balcony. The unusual shape of the columns, tapering from a 20 foot in diameter pad down to a delicate 9-inch shoe, draws attention to the flow of empty space around them, so that the space itself becomes dynamic. From this point on, curves would become predominant in Wright's designs.

Taliesin West
Scottsdale, Arizona, 1938
Wright's residence and studio in Scottsdale, Arizona was a crowning part of his triumphant hat trick of major works in the 1930s. Taliesin is so much an organic part of its site that it seems to have been formed by a force of nature. The low, ground-hugging silhouette, and unobtrusive walls of poured concrete and native stone blend imperceptibly into the landscape.

Taliesin West
Bell Tower and Pergola
Taliesin West is plotted along diagonal lines, in the informal style of Wright's earlier Ocotillo Desert Camp (1929) in Chandler, Arizona. The large oak trusses in this picture echo the diagonal "footprint" or basic layout of the building. It was appropriate for an architect's home and work-space that the central motif so strongly resembled a draughtsman's triangle!

Taliesin West
Wright's third great creation in this extraordinarily rich decade of work was his own studio in Phoenix: Taliesin West, completed in 1938. Wright called the site on a desert mesa twenty-six miles from the capital a "look over the rim of the world." Concrete walls made of cement and large pieces of local rock supported deeply cantilevered redwood roof rafters covered with stretched linen canvas. The canvas was adequate protection from the sun and from flash storms in the desert, as well as the cold nights. In the new setting, Wright felt his imagination liberated by "an aesthetic, even ascetic, idealization of space, of breadth and height and of strange firm forms."

The foundation of red desert stone and the low-lying lightweight superstructure meld imperceptibly into the scrub and cactus landscape. Inner pools and gardens give the effect of a sheltered oasis. There is a dialectical tension between the airy outer structure of

wood and canvas and the chthonic power of cave-like inner masonry at the core of the building. In the workroom, the redwood trusswork plunges like enormous draftsman's triangles next to the tables, echoing the beautiful "abstract forest" of oak-beam trusswork at the Hillside School Building in Spring Green, Wisconsin. Overall, the building appears to have been scooped out of the desert rather than merely built upon it. Seven set-back mesalike terraces provide vantages for views of the surrounding country.

Taliesin West
Living Room

Olgivanna and Frank Lloyd Wright found a true oasis in the desert at Taliesin West. Olgivanna liked the change from Wisconsin winters—"This is such a different world from Wisconsin—like another planet," she told Wright. She cherished the fragile desert blossoms of staghorn cactus, prickly pear and ocotillo. For his part, Wright prized the miles-long desert views, which he called "an esthetic, even ascetic, idealization of space."

Taliesin West
Interior

The roof of the original structure at Taliesin West consisted of movable canvas panels, so that in effect the drafting room became a kind of plein-air studio, open to the influence of the desert. The airy, open ceiling recalled the canvas tents of the building's origins in a desert camp, and contrasted dramatically with the rooted-ness and solidity of the massive masonry foundations.

The Usonian Houses

Wright was fairly brimming with ideas in the 1930s. Broadacre City was Wright's name for a grandiose restructuring of American cities that would "exist every-where and nowhere." Mainly it existed on paper, and reflected the flight to the suburbs that was already taking place in America, with or without Wright. As Henry Ford, maker of the machine that made the shift possible, put it, "we shall solve the City Problem by leaving the city." At the same time, Wright was developing the pro-totype of an idealized American home on a budget, which would become an influential and much-copied reality.

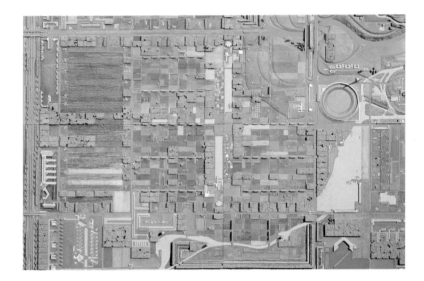

Broadacre City
Project, 1935

In some respects, Wright's grandiose plans for Broadacre City were a channel for his ambitions in the absence of commissions in the early 1930s. This model owed perhaps more than Wright would like to admit to Le Corbusier's concept of a Garden City in his Ville Radieuse plan for Paris in 1925. Both men were at heart anti-urbanists, rather than great urban thinkers. More contemporary critics such as Jane Jacobs realized that it was precisely the density of street life that Wright and Le Corbusier sought to eliminate that made great cities so vital.

Paul R. and Jean S. Hanna House, (Honeycomb House)
Palo Alto, California, 1937

The Honeycomb House, named for its design based on hexagonal shapes, was one of the grander Usonians. The obtuse, 120-degree angles of the hexagons opened up the interior in radical new ways, so that the viewer is put in a dynamic, ever-shifting relationship with the space. The hallmarks of Usonian design were economical, modular con-struction and open floor plans, but Wright extended the concept, in the way he constantly experimented with the basic Prairie Style.

The first Usonian House—as Wright called it, after Usonia, his own name for the United States—was the Herbert Jacobs House (1937) in Madison, Wisconsin. Five distinct types of Usonian Houses have been identified, but they share common features of an open floor plan with a central kitchen and adjacent dining and living areas, a secluded bedroom zone, and an underlying geometrical grid pattern. The houses were heated by steam or hot-water pipes radiating up from a thin concrete floor, and many used prefabricated walls. Wright devel-

oped some stunning variations, such as the hexagonally plotted Honeycomb House for Paul R. Hanna in Palo Alto, California, in which the walls meet at obtuse angles.

A 1940 retrospective of Wright's work at the Museum of Modern Art in New York honored the renaissance of Wright's "second career" with models and drawings of Fallingwater, the Johnson Administration Building, and the Jacobs House. But the Frank Lloyd Wright show was by no means over. The renowned architect saved some of his boldest work for last.

Herbert F. Johnson House (Wingspread)
Racine, Wisconsin, 1939
Wingspread is considered to be the last of the Prairie Houses. It was the largest residence Wright ever built, and is a fascinating example of the transition to curvilinear forms in his later work. After Wingspread, Wright concentrated his residential work on the more modestly scaled Usonian Houses, while his commercial projects explored new realms of abstract space.

Wingspread
Living Room
Wingspread's centerpiece is a curvilinear, free-standing, four-sided hearth. The space in the room is in constant flux, upward along the narrow yet massive column of the hearth, and outward along the tiered skylights, arrayed like spreading wings. The hearth, a central symbol in all of Wright's residences, is a signpost of his departure into the use of curved space.

Later Works

The last stage of Wright's career was a combination of thrifty recycling of old, unused projects and extraordinary developments in designs based on circular forms. The crystalline shape of Wright's grandiose Steel Cathedral, meant to be taller than any building in New York when it was planned in 1926, found a more modest and pleasing expression in the Beth Sholom Synagogue in Elkins Park, Pennsylvania, completed in 1959.

An innovative tower structure with floors cantilevered from a deeply anchored "tap root" that Wright proposed for the St. Marks-in-the-Bouwerie Towers in 1931 appeared in the Price Building (1956) in Bartleby, Oklahoma, one of Wright's handful of tall structures.

A 1956 project for a branchlike, mile-high skyscraper with atomic-powered elevators in Chicago remains only a tantalizing sketch.

H.C. Price Company Tower
Bartlesville, Oklahoma, 1956
In contradistinction to Wright's view that a building should be organically related to its site, the Price Tower has next to nothing to do with its environs of a small Western city—in fact it was originally designed for New York City. However, the 19-story tower of concrete, glass, and copper loses none of its delicate, sculptural charm—a skyscraper that manages to look small.

Beth Sholom Synagogue
Elkins Park, Pennsylvania, 1959
Ever thrifty in recycling his unused projects, Wright scaled down his grandiose plan for the 1,500-foot tall Steel Cathedral of 1926, meant to be the tallest modern building in the world, to the more esthetically pleasing Beth Sholom Synagogue.

Beth Sholom Synagogue
Interior
The airy structure of concrete, steel, glass, fiberglass, and oiled walnut is suspended from a triangular frame that does away with any internal supports to create a soaring inner space of pure light. Wright's embracing Transcendentalist views spoke to all faiths.

Norman Lykes House
Phoenix, Arizona, 1959
Though designed in 1959, the Lykes House was not constructed until 1968, and was the last residential design by Wright to be built. Made of gorgeously-colored desert-rose concrete block and Philippine mahogany, the house, based on circular segments, is fully integrated with the desert environment, yet seems to alight like a marvelous abstraction on its hillside site.

Annunciation Greek Orthodox Church
Wauwatosa, Wisconsin, 1956
The great concrete drum of the Annunciation Greek Orthodox Church seems to be drawn from some otherworldly inspiration, as it perches like a brightly decorative flying saucer on the open landscape. The church represents the transition towards purely sculptural forms in Wright's later work.

Following page:
Guggenheim Museum
Rotunda
The interior of the Guggenheim is Transcendentalism in action, one of the great experiences in world architecture. The force of space becomes manifest in the ever-changing spiralling compositions and interrelationships of the helical ramp leading up to a skylit dome. Swirling space itself seems to provide the shape of the container.

The Guggenheim Museum

The Solomon R. Guggenheim Museum in New York (1959), probably Wright's most familiar landmark, seems sui generis, like a flying saucer that landed among the staid granite fronts of Fifth Avenue. But antecedents of the quarter-mile-long spiral ramp that gives the Guggenheim its form can be seen in sketches for the exuberant car ramp for the Roy Wetmore Automobile Showroom project (1948) and the spiral ramps of the Self-Service Garage project in Pittsburgh (1949). Precursors can also be seen in the ramp for the Mercedes-Benz Showroom (1954) in Manhattan, and more loftily in the V. C. Morris Gift Shop (1949) in San Francisco as well as the David Wright House (1952). Wright's venture into spiral forms reflected his uncritical love of the automobile.

While the Guggenheim clearly has deficiencies as an art museum—from a structure that simply overpowers the exhibits to the difficulty of hanging paintings on curved, sloping walls and, further, to the awkwardness of observers standing with one leg higher than the other to view art—despite these factors, the Guggenheim is one of the most exhilarating spaces in the world of architecture.

The entry through low revolving doors followed by the glorious uprush of the inverted conical volume of space is a remarkable and unforgettable experience. The space is in constant flow, uninterrupted by posts, beams, or rectangular forms. Every small change in vantage point alters the experience of the space, from the hemi-cyclic slices of the terraces seen directly across to the complex, rhythmic framings of the domed skylight. The exterior is a true reflection of the inner space, making it an "architecture of the within," in Wright's phrase.

Guggenheim Museum

The Guggenheim violates many of Wright's precepts—it has nothing to do with its site among the granite matrons of Fifth Avenue, and is in many respects woefully inadequate as a museum space for displaying art, yet it endures as an icon of the creative power of modern art.

Solomon R. Guggenheim Museum

New York City, 1959

The inverted ziggurat of the Guggenheim Museum, which looks as if it had been cast on some celestial potter's wheel, is Wright's boldest statement of the form of a building as a container of space. The vortex quality of space is amplified in such details as the whip-like exterior service ramp that seems to throw off lines of force. Porthole-like windows at street level pick up the circular plan of the building's footprint, and in view of Wright's emphatic anticontextualism, give the building the sense of a spaceship.

Marin County Civic Center
San Rafael, California, 1962
The Marin County Civic Center
is a vision of how art can play a
role in public life. It is wonderfully
human and approachable for a state
building. The structure is enormous,
but does not seem so, sinuously
following the contours of its hillside
setting. Wright's later works tend
to be given short shrift critically,
but the Marin building is a mature
and evocative expression of his
comprehension of space and
the role of humankind in nature.

The Marin County Civic Center

Wright's last major commission, the posthumously completed Marin County Civic Center in San Rafael, California, (1962) is stunningly sculptural, unabashedly decorative, and unusually personal for a government office. The only thing comparable is Le Corbusier's sculpturally curved concrete buildings for the government in Chandigarh, India.

The building is massive, yet human-scaled. The skylit mall beyond the immense low ceiling of the entryway is airy and inviting, dating back to the plan of the Larkin Building. Outside, the sleek double ovals and connecting dome become a part of the rounded hillside setting. The cheerful arcuated front combines form and function, yet rejects Modernism's austerity.

Frank Lloyd Wright died at home, at Taliesin West, at the age of ninety-one on April 9, 1959, from a coronary thrombosis following an operation. A Unitarian minister read the 121st Psalm at the funeral, whose last verse seems to reflect Wright's view of the continuity of space: "The Lord shall preserve thy going out and thy coming in from this time forth, and even for evermore."

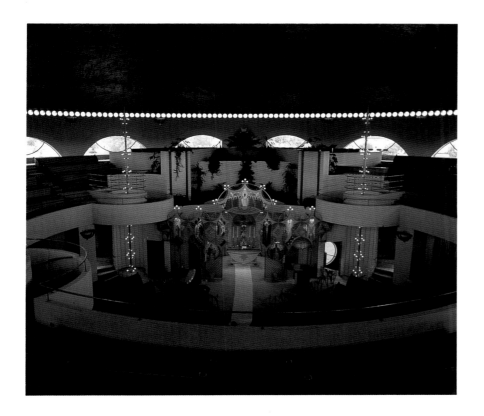

Annunciation Greek Orthodox Church
Interior
Though radically sculptural in conception, the Annunciation church is based on a circular plan, an archetypal symbol of unity and continuity. Interior and exterior form an organic whole, with blue seats mirroring the blue ceramic-tile roof, and the central circle motif repeated and amplified by the round balcony, the hemispheric upper windows and the space within the sheltering dome.

V. C. Morris Gift Shop
San Francisco, 1949
Everything is in motion in Wright's later work. The grandly unscrolling spiral ramp in the Morris Gift Shop in San Francisco is a precursor of Wright's design for the Guggenheim Museum, where the outer shape would express the space contained within. Wright's use of spirals and ramps can be traced directly to his love of automobiles. A giant ramp makes an early appearance in his 1925 project for the Gordon Strong Automobile Objective and Planetarium and later in a 1948 project for the Roy Wetmore Automobile Showroom.

CODA

In February of 1995, thirty-six years after Wright died, and fifty-seven years after the original proposal, the city of Madison in Wisconsin, proceeded with the construction of Monona Terrace, a visionary civic complex on the shore of Lake Monona. The convention center is planned to open July 4, 1997.

Wright designed the forty-four-acre complex in 1938 but it was stalled by a series of financial and political setbacks. A rendering of Monona Terrace, done in the 1950s, shows a glass-walled pavilion set between solid towers with low arches—reminiscent of the Marin County Building—and spiral parking ramps. It has the potential to be one of Wright's great works, with a play between enclosing and expressing space in the juxtaposition of its glass and solid towers.

If anything is dated about the building perhaps it is the cheerful optimism of the spiral parking ramps——in an age that has become more cynical about the effects of the automobile on urban development. The two ball-bearing shapes on top, so expressive of the organic unity of the machine age, now appear like postmodern maraschino cherries on a cake top.

The building's lasting contribution, like much of Wright's most magnificent work, may be the harmony it appears to project with its chosen site. The wave-shaped arches of the circular glass wall will merge the shadowed interior with the sparkling lakefront, avoiding the monotony of uninspired glass-curtain buildings. Wright's last great work is a shining example through time of how site and structure, nature and architecture are one.

Mile High Illinois

Project, 1956

Wright's plan for a mind-bending mile-high skyscraper in Chicago was really more along the lines of a thought experiment, just to see if it could be done. The glass-curtained tower would achieve its height by using a deep tap root core to anchor it in the ground. Even in his most meglomaniacal schemes, Wright showed a sensitive use of organic forms, such as the branch-like asymmetrical angles of the Mile High Illinois.

Monona Terrace
Madison, Wisconsin, completion date 1997
A 1992 rendition by Taliesin Architects, the successor firm to
Frank Lloyd Wright's practice after his death, shows the high arched
windows of the convention center looking out over Lake Monona,
flanked by massive rounded towers with low arched entryways
in the manner of the Marin County building. Wright continues
to be a vital and creative force in American architecture.

INDEX